Coloring the Silence

Text © 2017 Sandy Eisenberg Sasso
Illustrations © 2017 Jessica M. Springman

First edition
Published by Westminster John Knox Press
Louisville, Kentucky

17 18 19 20 21 22 23 24 25 26—10 9 8 7 6 5 4 3 2 1

Book design by Allison Taylor
Cover design by Allison Taylor
Cover illustration: Jessica M. Springman

Thank you for purchasing this book of reflections and art. Each piece of art was individually hand-drawn specifically for use in this work by artist Jessica M. Springman of Indianapolis, Indiana. We hope that you enjoy these authentic and inspiring pieces.

ISBN: 978-0-664-26306-5 (paperback)

∞ The paper used in this publication meets the minimum requirements of the American National Standard for Information Sciences— Permanence of Paper for Printed Library Materials, ANSI Z39.48-1992.

Most Westminster John Knox Press books are available at special quantity discounts when purchased in bulk by corporations, organizations, and special-interest groups. For more information, please e-mail SpecialSales@wjkbooks.com.

Coloring the Silence

AN ADULT COLORING BOOK FOR REFLECTION

Sandy Eisenberg Sasso

Illustrations by
Jessica M. Springman

WJK WESTMINSTER
JOHN KNOX PRESS
LOUISVILLE · KENTUCKY

On Silence

Legend tells us that at the time of the giving of the Ten Commandments, no bird sang and no fowl flew,

no ox bellowed and no lion growled, no angel stirred a wing.

The sea did not roar; the wind did not whistle; no creature spoke a word.

And when all was silent, a divine voice came forth.

Silence isn't just the absence of noise.

It is the deep quiet place we go

when all praise and censure stops—

our own and others—

and our soul takes a breath.

Color that silence.

On Blessing Our Children

May you be a person of character,

strong, but not unbending,

gentle, but not weak.

Wherever you journey, may your steps be firm and

may you walk in just paths and not be afraid.

When you speak, let your words be words of wisdom and friendship.

Whatever you do, may you act with loving-kindness, humility, and generosity.

May your hands build and your hearts preserve what is good and beautiful in our world.

May you build a family, a rich heritage to which to belong,

and from that sacred place may you be connected to all who dwell on earth.

What is your sacred place?

On Living Fully

Discover joy in music, delight in books, and enchantment in art.

Ask lots of questions, find pleasure in ambiguity,

and now and again choose the unpaved path.

Laugh until you are all laughter,

sing until you are all song,

and love until you are all love.

Think of times you laughed, sang, loved fully.

What questions are you asking in your life?

On Pilgrimage

We often think of pilgrimages as going up,

climbing to a higher place.

But on mountaintops the air is so thin, it's hard to breathe.

What's below appears so small, you can forget it is real.

The ascent may take your breath away,

but it is the descending that's hard;

it's too easy to slip with no one to catch your fall.

I'm weary of mountains where we're always looking up

or looking down and sacrificing,

so our neck hurts and we need glasses.

Our feet upon the mountains are blistered,

and our shoes are always wrong—not enough "soul."

There is another kind of pilgrimage:

Sitting by a river,

gathering at a well,

where we wash our feet

and catch our breath

and our soul.

Where are the places that you catch your breath and your soul?

On Being Delayed

When we are going somewhere, the way often seems like an inconvenience.

Waiting in airports, in lines, for the "next available representative"

is a waste of our time.

We have important work to do, and we are in a hurry.

We get lost, delayed, cut off. We are angry.

We simply want to get to the point, to our destination.

But what if the point isn't our destination?

What if the appointment is along the way, in-between?

What detour in your life ended up being a blessing?

On Growing Older

Every age we decide how we want to be known:

Sometimes wise; at times foolish.

Sometimes agreeable; at times rebellious.

Sometimes serious; at times playful.

May we reach an old age remembering

to dance without being embarrassed,

to sing, even if out of tune,

without forgetting

to laugh, to dream,

and still to hope.

How do you want to be known?

On Compassion
(on Genesis 22)

In the world to come
no one will take Isaac
up a mountain
and leave him
alone.

The angel stopped Abraham
then left
without a word to Isaac,
and God
never spoke to Abraham again.

The ram turned to ashes
was no comfort.
The fire died
cold on the mountain;
only scent of smoke remained.

In the world to come,
I will not leave you
there
on a mountain
alone.

I will wrap you
in soft blankets
of lamb's wool
until you stop
trembling.

I will bring water
and rock you,
rock you,
rock you
until you sleep.

In the world to come,
I will carry you down the mountain,
heart beating like angels' wings,
shofar sounding,
and you laughing again.

When have you felt alone?
Who carried you?
Who have you carried?

On Uselessness

What if we were to realize that no moment was meaningless, unless we squandered it?

What if we were to act as if there were no insignificant places, unless we overlooked them?

What if we were to speak as if there were no empty words, unless we spoke them carelessly?

What if we were to believe that there were no useless things, unless we treated them uselessly?

How would our lives change?

On Balance

I believe that opposites are best when matched:
love and power, justice and compassion, faith and doubt,
seriousness and play, religion and spirit.

Love without power is sentimentality.
Justice without compassion is cruel.
Faith without doubt is dishonest. Doubt without faith is cynicism.
Seriousness without play is boring and unimaginative.
Religion without spirit is dead.

Red without yellow knows no orange, the color of happiness.
And God, God is the "and" that brings those opposites into one harmonious whole.

Colors that are opposite each other on the color wheel are complementary.
They remind us of the beauty of balance.

What is out of balance in your life?
Where do you need to add the "and"?

On Memory

I wonder who we are when our memory starts to go,

when all that we knew and felt begins to dim.

The shadows are there; we can still see them.

We reach out to touch them, to bring them back.

Yet they escape every time we try to take hold.

What happens when those we love can't form new memories or retrieve old ones,

when everything passes like water through a sieve?

The poet says every person is a dam between past and future,

but I don't know what happens when the dam breaks.

All I know is how the heart breaks.

And all the memories come in a gushing torrent

and reside with us

who still remember.

What memories do you hold in trust?

On Creativity

We are all creators.
We breathe in what is—
a chaotic swirl of smells and tastes,
sights and sounds, words and more words—
and we breathe out form.

We consider what is not—
failure and loss.
And out of emptiness and absence
we fashion something original:
a world.

What are you creating?

On Prayer

Don't be fooled into thinking that all it takes to pray is fingers clasped
and eyes cast to the sky.

Prayer is more about outstretched hands than folded ones.
It's more about looking around at the world than up at the heavens.

All people pray, even if they deny it.
Give voice to your deepest regret and your greatest hope;
speak your worst fear and your greatest joy.
That is prayer.

What do you regret?
What do you hope?

On Friendship

Legend tells us that each person carries a light visible only from the world above.

When two people meet and become friends, their single lights are united as one.

From that union an angel is born.

But if friends grow distant and separate, the angel born of their union weeps

and begins to waste away.

It is able to survive for only one year, and then it dies.

But we can revive the angel.

When two people meet after a year of separation and grow close again,

they breathe life into the dying angel.

When that happens, you can feel the faint brush of wings.

Then you will know that the angel has been reborn.

What friendships have you neglected?

How might you reconnect?

On Anger, Cain, and Abel

You could see from their features
that they were related.
Adam's high forehead and Eve's wide eyes.

First friends,
no one else to talk with
when Mom and Dad didn't understand.

First playmates,
telling secrets, playing hide-and-seek
among the acacia bushes.

No one remembers them that way,
chubby hands wrapping Eve's finger,
sounds of brothers' deep, belly laughs.

We need to see them as before.
Enough portraits of slaughter,
enough blood splattering white canvas.

Who made Abel fair-haired and clean-shaven?
Cain with beard and shadow?
Dark beast against golden boy?

Paint Cain, head bowed, knees bent,
in the earth, planting red anemones.

Picture Abel, head raised, standing tall,
wrestling sheep, composing soft melodies.

It is the same old chorus, Cain and Abel,
Isaac and Ishmael, Jacob and Esau.

Hurling stones, waging war.
Someone always dies;
someone's always exiled.

They were brothers—remember?
Laughing boys—recall?

We need to see them before the offering,
before the anger, before the murder,
in order to find our way back there—again.

What do you need to remember in order to let go of your anger?

On Brokenness

The first tablets of the Ten Commandments were said to have been written by the finger of God. But Moses, upon seeing his people worshiping the Golden Calf, broke those stone tablets. Where were they placed? Legend tells us that the second set of tablets, written by the hand of Moses, was placed along with the broken ones inside the Holy Ark.

The ark, like the human heart, contains both what is broken and what is whole—rejection and acceptance, doubt and faith.

The shattered fragments and questions, the loss and pain of our lives remain with us. Hard as we might, we cannot easily discard or bury them out of sight. Yet they do not have to be a burden weighing us down, imprisoning us. They can be the pieces that give our lives meaning and make us whole. We can repair what is broken.

The Japanese have a practice called *kintsugi* by which they repair damaged vessels by using gold, silver, and platinum to bind together what has been fractured. The cracks are visible, making the restored piece even more beautiful than the original.

What is broken in your life that you are trying to hide?
How might you, in acknowledging it, also transform it?

On Losses

Legend describes an Angel of Losses. Her name is "The One Who Knows."

She gropes in the places of deep darkness, in the valley of shadows, to recapture what time has lost.

She searches with a light, a small candle flame to find and remember the souls

of those who have died and been forgotten.

With that flame she rekindles the glow of those souls and keeps in memory all that has vanished.

Through that light of remembrance, we recover what we have lost.

In the shadows, in the absence of color, we discover

new shades and pigments with which to paint our world.

When was a time of deep darkness and loss for you?

In the shadows, what color do you find to paint the world?

On God's Name

The whole earth is filled with God's glory, but I do not know Its name.

"I don't know why I want to name God an 'Old Warm Bathrobe,'" a woman announced. One year later, she found her answer. Her mother died, and she took her old, warm bathrobe and wrapped it around her and felt the presence of God.

I do not know Its name, but I think It must wrap around us like an old, warm bathrobe.

A young intelligence officer returned home from Iraq. He didn't talk much about the war. He said, "I want to call God 'My Trampoline.' It is what allows me to bounce back after falling down."

I do not know Its name, but I think It must feel like a young man flying.

A five-year-old boy, said, "I want to call God 'Healer.'" His mother was dying of breast cancer. I do not know Its name, but I think it must sound like that little boy praying.

"And what do you think God's name is?" a dad asked his son. Sitting on his father's lap, the boy said, "I think God's name is 'Between.'"

I do not know Its name, but I think it must be somewhere between a son and his dad.

"Do not be confused if you hear many voices, know that I am one and the same. I will be what I will be. I will become what I will become. This is my name forever."

What is your name for God?
What color feels sacred today?

On Hope

In the ancient Temple in Jerusalem, there was a special lamp called the eternal light.

It was to burn continuously. But I imagine that it didn't.

Sometimes a wind must have blown it out. Sometimes the oil must have run out.

So I think that it is called the eternal light not because it burned forever,

but because if it did go out,

it could be rekindled.

What lights in your life need rekindling?

On Slowing Down

An Amish man noticed a cyclist speeding past the cool shade of trees in order to catch up to his fellow cyclists.

The man was perspiring and panting.

The Amish man called out to him,

"My friend, you pass too quickly through the shadows."

In what ways do you need to slow down?

On Dreams

What if the places we avoid,

the questions we evade,

the things we fear

are where the holy dwells?

Find the courage to take the risk.

Stand on uncommon and unsteady ground.

Let blessing surprise you.

What places or questions are you avoiding?

On Getting through the Dark

On their first day in the Garden of Eden, Adam and Eve ate from the Tree of Knowledge of Good and Evil. That night the sun continued to shine in honor of the beginning of the Sabbath. Sunlight remained throughout the seventh day. But at that day's end, the sun began to sink below the horizon. Adam and Eve were greatly afraid. They believed the setting of the sun was their fault. Before long, all warmth and light vanished, and it seemed to them that the dark was the end of the world.

Legend tells us that it was at that moment that God provided Adam and Eve with two stones. They struck them together and created a flame. The flame became a fire, and the fire helped them get through the dark night. In the morning, the sun rose again. The first couple realized that the setting of the sun and its rising were just the way of the world. They blessed the day and the night.

Think of a time when you were afraid, when you believed that everything was your fault, that there was no light ahead. What helped you get through the night?

On Light

We have a name for when day fades into night and a name for when night just opens into morning. We call the lights that are neither day nor night *dusk* and *dawn*. These are the delicate boundaries, where one time blends into the other. They are the fragile margins, where light scatters, where blue sky morphs into the reds and oranges of sunset and sunrise.

At dusk, the weariness and pollution of the day often fade colors to pale yellow and pink. At dawn, having spent the night in darkness, we see more clearly the bright reds and oranges of a sunrise.

We also have a name for the light that is neither sun nor moon, where one generation folds into another. It is the light of the first day of creation. And a spark of that primordial light is called a *soul*, and it never dies. Its color is brighter than anything visible to the human eye. Sometimes we see it best after we have been in the dark.

If you look deep inside yourself, you will find that light.

What color is the light of the first day of creation?

What prevents you from seeing that light?

What dark time allowed you to see more clearly?

On Trying New Things

Don't be afraid to try something new, something challenging.

Don't worry, others aren't watching you.

They are too busy paying attention to themselves.

If you never risk being embarrassed, failing,

if you always play it safe,

you'll miss the opportunity to do something grand.

What is something new that you have been afraid to try?

On What Makes You Beautiful

There is a spark that you carry. It is what makes you beautiful.

You won't find that spark by looking in the mirror.

You will find it by looking into yourself and looking out for others.

Sometimes when you are afraid and uncertain,

another person's spark will light the way for you,

just as your spark will be there for others.

Recognize the spark you carry and the sparks that others have.

The flame you create is beautiful.

Who has been a light for you?

For whom have you been a light?

On Being Stuck

There are gates that open in our lives,
but we are hesitant to walk through.
We feel stuck.
It is as though there are guards
who keep us from entering.
Those guards have names.
They are Doubt, Pride, and Fear.

Doubt is a pessimist.
It tells us that we are too old,
too weak, too inferior to begin again.
Doubt is agnostic.
There is no proof of God,
so why search for transcendence?
We'll never achieve it anyway.

Pride is a cynic.
It expands our ego and contracts our conscience.
It tells us to take all we can, before someone else does.
Pride is an atheist.
There is no God,
so why waste our time seeking meaning
when there is none?

Fear is a naysayer.
It tells us not to risk being truthful or vulnerable.
Judgment by others is painful, our own even more so.
Fear is faithless.
It believes that there might be a way to find the sacred,
but it is too dangerous to try.

Remember—the gates are open.
Remember—you can face doubt, pride, and fear,
conquer all that keeps you from feeling stuck,
and enter the open gates.

What in your life keeps you from entering the gates?

Old Lab   12 pm   June 15
F.C.   June 8th   aft 12 pm
Sam,   Job 1   8/15

13y Math
8-8 pm

9 780664 263065